Learning Short-take®

MANAGING ORGANIZATIONAL CHANGE

Tools to help your team through change

CATHERINE MATTISKE

TPC - The Performance Company Pty Ltd
Level 20, Darling Park
Tower 2, 201 Sussex Street,
Sydney NSW 2000
Australia

ACN 077 455 273
email: tpc@tpc.net.au
Website: www.catherinemattiske.com

© TPC – The Performance Company Pty Limited
First edition published in 2006
Second edition published in 2011
Third edition published in 2022

All rights reserved. Apart from any fair dealing for the purposes of study, research or review, as permitted under Australian copyright law, no part of this publication may be reproduced by any means without the written permission of the copyright owner. Every effort has been made to obtain permission relating to information reproduced in this publication.

The information in this publication is based on the current state of commercial and industry practice, applicable legislation, general law and the general circumstances as at the date of publication. No person shall rely on any of the contents of this publication and the publisher and the author expressly exclude all liability for direct and indirect loss suffered by any person resulting in any way from the use of or reliance on this publication or any part of it. Any options and advice are offered solely in pursuance of the author's and the publisher's intention to provide information, and have not been specifically sought.

For eBook version: By payment of the required fees, you have been granted the non-exclusive, non-transferable right to access and read the text of this e-book on screen. No part of this text may be reproduced, transmitted, downloaded, decompiled, reverse engineered, or stored in or introduced into any information storage retrieval system, in any form or by any means, whether the electronic or mechanical, now known or hereinafter invented, without the express permission of the author.

A catalogue record for this book is available from the National Library of Australia

National Library of Australia
Cataloguing-in-Publication data

Mattiske, Catherine
Managing Organizational Change: Tools to help your team through change

ISBN 978-1-921547-15-7

1. Occupational training 2. Learning I. Title

370.113

Distributed by TPC - The Performance Company - www.catherinemattiske.com
For further information contact TPC - The Performance Company, Sydney Australia on +61 (02) 9555 1953.

HELLO.

Welcome to the Learning Short-take® process!

This Learning Short-take® is a bite sized learning package that aims to improve your skills and provide you with an opportunity for personal and professional development to achieve success in your role.

This Learning Short-take® combines self study with workplace activities in a unique learning system to keep you motivated and energized. So let's get started!

Step 1:
What's inside?

- Learning Short-take®. This section contains all of the learning content and will guide you through the learning process.
- Learning Activities. You will be prompted to complete these as you read through.
- Learning Journal. This is a summary of your key learnings. Update it when prompted.
- Skill Development Action Plan. Learning is about taking action. This is your action plan where you'll plan how you will implement your learning.

Step 2:
Complete the Learning Short-take®

- Learning Short-takes® are best completed in a quiet environment that is free of distractions.
- Schedule time in your calendar to complete the Learning Short-take® and prioritize this time as an investment in your own professional development.
- Depending on the title, most participants complete the Learning Short-take® from 90 minutes to 2.5 hours.

Step 3:
Meet with your Manager/Coach

- Schedule a 30 minute meeting with your Manager or Coach.
- At this meeting share your completed Activities, Learning Journal and Skill Development Action Plan.
- Most importantly, discuss and agree on how you will implement your learning in your role.

GET VIP ACCESS
TO YOUR MATERIALS

This Learning Short-take® includes an interactive activity book, associated tools and job aids, plus a bonus eBook.

1 Visit https://www.catherinemattiske.com/books

2 Select your book

3 Click: **VIP ACCESS**

4 Enter the code: MOC2022266

WELCOME

Managing Organizational Change
Tools to help your team through change

Managing Organizational Change provides managers and leaders with the tools and techniques to lead in a changing environment. This Learning Short-take® includes a series of realistic workplace activities to assist in identifying the reactions to change within your team, and guides you through the steps to influence team members, to gain agreement and implement change.

Managing the challenge of change is a powerful responsibility. Making the investment of time, energy and money to implement the change successfully will benefit everyone - the employees, management, and the organization. Advocates of change will enhance the implementation and installation of change. Employees will return your investment in them with increased productivity, higher motivation, and personal growth.

Managing Organizational Change includes the **Strategic Change Implementation Worksheet**, provided as a free downloadable tool.

Now let's get started!

1	Learning Short-take® > Start here
2	Learning Journal 77
3	Skill Development Action Plan 83
4	Quick Reference 89
5	Next Steps 107

© 2022, TPC - The Performance Company Pty Limited. All rights reserved.

"
"Unless you are prepared to give up something valuable you will never be able to truly change at all, because you'll be forever in the control of things you can't give up."

ANDY LAW, CREATIVE COMPANY

Section 1

LEARNING SHORT-TAKE®

WHAT'S IN THIS LEARNING SHORT-TAKE®

"Whosoever desires constant success must change his conduct with the times."

NICCOLO MACHIAVELLI

Table of Contents

How to Complete Your Learning Short-take®	5
Activity Checklist	6
Learning Objectives	7
Let's Get Started	8
Part 1 - Understanding Organizational Change	11
Why Manage Change?	18
Responsibility for Managing Change	21
Part 2 - Planning Change	25
Strategies for Implementing Change - The 8 Steps	26
Part 3 - Understanding your Employees	33
Understanding your Employees	34
Change Reaction	36
Part 4 - Successfully Implementing Change	43
Three Key Change Management Skills	44
Change Resistance	47
Part 5 - Working with The Change Matrix	53
Working with The Change Matrix	54
Tips & Traps of Managing Change	62
Building an Enthusiastic Team	65
Part 6 - A Final Thought	75
The Crow and the Pitcher	76

HOW TO COMPLETE YOUR LEARNING SHORT-TAKE®

1. **Reflect on your skills and abilities** in managing organizational change and how you use this information to improve effectiveness in your role.

2. **Complete the Initial Skills Self-Assessment**.

3. Highlight specific skill areas that you believe you could develop more. Add these to the **Learning Journal**. Add to your Learning Journal as you go.

4. When you have completed this Learning Short-take® **meet with your Manager/Coach**. In this meeting, you will jointly establish a personal **Skill Development Action Plan**.

5. **Subject to your coach's final review** and assessment, you will either sign off the module, or undertake further skill development as appropriate.

"Your success in life isn't based on your ability to simply change. It is based on your ability to change faster than your competition, customers and business."

MARK SANBORN

ACTIVITY CHECKLIST

During this Learning Short-take® you will be prompted to complete the following activities:

- Activity 1 - Initial Skills Self-Assessment 9
- Activity 2 - Business Challenges Worksheet 17
- Activity 3 - Managing Organizational Change - Case Study 22
- Activity 4 - Strategies for Managing Change 30
- Activity 5a - The Change Matrix - Assessing Employees 41
- Activity 5b - The Change Matrix - Plotting Employees 42
- Activity 6 - Reflection Exercise 45
- Activity 7 - Preparing for Change Resistance 51
- Activity 8 - Managing The Change Matrix 72
- Learning Journal 77
- Skill Development Action Plan 83

"Change is the law of life and those who look only to the past or present are certain to miss the future."

JOHN F. KENNEDY

LEARNING OBJECTIVES

After you have completed this Learning Short-take®, you should be able to:

- Identify your role in the **change process**.
- Learn how to identify and address the **human face of change**, and overcome **emotional and intellectual** challenges.
- Take action in overcoming **performance barriers**.
- Build confidence in getting your team **through the change and beyond**.
- Create a Skill Development Action Plan

"Company cultures are like country cultures. Never try to change one. Try, instead, to work with what you've got."

PETER DRUCKER

LET'S GET STARTED

Managing the challenge of change is a powerful responsibility. It is not easy and it is often expensive. However, failing to recognise the need to change and not working to build commitment to the change is far more costly.

Making the investment of time, energy and money will benefit everyone - the employee, management, and the organization.

Advocates of change will enhance its implementation and installation. Employees will return your investment in them with increased productivity and personal growth.

This Learning Short-take® will assist you to manage organizational change by identifying the reactions to change within your team, lead you through the steps to individual acceptance, and help you produce the results you desire.

 **Complete Activity # 1**
Initial Skills Self-Assessment

ACTIVITY 1: INITIAL SKILLS SELF-ASSESSMENT

Understanding organizational change and how to manage it is critical to improving job and leadership success. This assessment covers the key skills in identifying and responding to change in order to improve individual and team performance.

Rate yourself on each of the techniques.
7   is competent and confident, little need for improvement
4   is average, needs improvement
1   is uncomfortable, major need for improvement

- Note specific areas of improvement related to each that you would like to develop. Be sure to include your **reasons** for your rating in each skill, as this reasoning will be a key part of the initial goal setting session with your coach.
- Start thinking about a personal development plan and identify two or three things you could do to improve your skills in this area and write them in the space provided.

I…	Rating	Reasoning
don't seek to control change, but rather to expect it, understand it, and manage it	1 2 3 4 5 6 7	
don't get wrapped up in doing "change for the sake of change", but know what goals I need to accomplish	1 2 3 4 5 6 7	
understand where the organization is currently, where it needs/wants to be, and how success will be measured	1 2 3 4 5 6 7	
only seek to implement change where it is realistic, achievable and measurable	1 2 3 4 5 6 7	
thoughtfully plan for and sensitively implement organizational change within my team	1 2 3 4 5 6 7	

ACTIVITY 1: CONTINUED

I...	Rating	Reasoning
treat people with humanity and respect and they reciprocate it	1 2 3 4 5 6 7	
communicate, involve, enable and facilitate involvement from affected people as early and as openly as possible	1 2 3 4 5 6 7	
check that people affected by the change agree with, or at least understand the need for change	1 2 3 4 5 6 7	
use face-to-face communication to handle sensitive aspects of the change process	1 2 3 4 5 6 7	
diffuse emotions, take a step back and encourage objectivity to enable sensible and constructive dialogue	1 2 3 4 5 6 7	
recognize and respond to the fact that people typically find change disturbing and threatening	1 2 3 4 5 6 7	
empower people to make decisions at a local operating level and delegate responsibility as much as possible	1 2 3 4 5 6 7	

Personal development plan ideas:

1

2

Now update your Learning Journal (page 77)

UNDERSTANDING ORGANIZATIONAL CHANGE

PART 1

UNDERSTANDING ORGANIZATIONAL CHANGE

> "The world doesn't fear a new idea. What it fears is a new experience."
>
> DH LAWRENCE

Typically, the concept of organizational change relates to **organization-wide changes** as opposed to smaller changes such as recruiting a new person or modifying a development program etc. Examples of organization-wide change include a change in vision or mission statement, restructuring initiatives, introducing new technologies, mergers, downsizing, re-engineering activities etc. Some experts refer to this type of change as **organizational transformation** where there is a **fundamental and radical reorientation in the way the organization operates**.

Change should not be done for the sake of change, but should be a robust strategy to achieve an identified organizational goal. Organizational change is **often provoked by some major external driving force** such as substantial budget reductions, the need for dramatic increases in productivity, or to address major new market opportunities.

Often, organizations undertake organizational change to **evolve to a different level in their life cycle**. For example, moving from a highly reactive entrepreneurial organization to a more stable and planned development. Transition to a **new style of management can also provoke organizational wide change** where new and unique personality types pervade the entire organization.

Most often there is **strong resistance** to organizational change. People are inherently afraid of the unknown, are often **cynical about the application** of change, and may doubt that the change will accomplish the desired organizational outcomes. The best approach to address resistance is through **increased and sustained communication and education** throughout the change process. Employees need to be able to **trust** the organization.

> *"The most successful businessman is the man who holds onto the old just as long as it is good, and grabs the new just as soon as it is better."*
>
> ROBERT P. VANDERPOEL

Organizational Change is today's Organizational Constant

Managing change is paramount for successfully implementing changes to organizational strategy, process, people and culture. More and more, staying competitive in the face of demographic trends, technological innovations, and globalization requires organizations to be more receptive to change than ever before.

Managing change well is a continuous and ongoing alignment of an organization's strategies, structures, and processes. A growing number of companies are undertaking the kinds of organizational changes needed to survive and prosper in today's environment.

- They are streamlining themselves and thereby becoming more agile and responsive to external demands.
- They are involving employees in key decisions and paying for performance rather than for time.
- They are proactively taking initiatives in innovating and managing change, rather than simply reacting to what has already happened.

Organization change is a strategic imperative in today's global, fast-paced environment. Unfortunately, often in the pursuit of change, trying to be the best, trying to stand out from the pack, and trying to seek higher and higher levels of status and power, managers and leaders in organizations impatiently clamor for the "latest and greatest" ideas. In their haste, they forget the fundamental and sound principles, which are pre-requisites

for a successfully change to occur and wonder why they are not making progress. Although managing change is difficult, implementing these few tried and true principles can help managers and leaders improve the organization's success.

Sources of Change: External vs. Internal Changes

There are two kinds of change:

1. Change as a result of **external influences** (like reductions in the economy or technological changes which affect the profitability or resources of an organization). We cannot control this type of change, but it does influence internal change.

2. Change as a result of **internal influences** (like restructuring or budget initiatives, which may drive the need for change). This type of change we can control.

Current Corporate Challenges

The following table lists six challenges facing most organizations today. Review this information in readiness for the following activity.

Financial Challenges	Globalization Challenges
<ul><li>Reducing operating costs to increase production efficiency</li><li>Developing and implementing business strategies that result in profitable return</li><li>Maintaining operating profits in an increasingly competitive business environment</li></ul>	<ul><li>New employee skills to deal with a global economy</li><li>Cultural issues</li><li>New ways of doing business</li></ul>
Recruiting Challenges	**Customer Challenges**
<ul><li>Attracting and retaining an appropriate number of qualified and competent staff</li><li>Filling key positions</li><li>Improving current employees</li></ul>	<ul><li>Ability to partner with customers</li><li>Helping customers understand how to shop and buy</li><li>Developing technology for greater customer satisfaction</li></ul>
Technology and Internet Challenges	**Corporate Knowledge Challenges**
<ul><li>Improving the use of technology to keep ahead of the competition</li><li>Gaining knowledge and implementing available technologies</li><li>Matching the latest technologies to customer requirements</li></ul>	<ul><li>Shared understanding of the organization's objectives</li><li>Command of products and services to deepen customer relationships</li><li>Open communication and linkages between and within departments</li></ul>

Complete Activity # 2
Business Challenges Worksheet

ACTIVITY 2: BUSINESS CHALLENGES WORKSHEET

Use this worksheet to compare the business challenges your company is facing. Add any business challenges that you see facing your organization that were not previously mentioned. Then indicate your own level of perceived importance for you organization using the scale from 1 to 5. Finally, list some ways you think you, as an internal performance consultant, might deal with these business challenges.

(1 = Not Important, 2= Somewhat Important, 3 = Important, 4 = Very Important, 5 = Extremely Important)

Business Challenges	Your perceived level of importance	Changes that will impact my role/team
Financial	1 2 3 4 5	
Recruiting	1 2 3 4 5	
Technology	1 2 3 4 5	
Knowledge Management	1 2 3 4 5	
Globalization	1 2 3 4 5	
Customer Satisfaction	1 2 3 4 5	
Other:	1 2 3 4 5	
Other:	1 2 3 4 5	

Now update your Learning Journal (page 77)

WHY MANAGE CHANGE?

Managing change means managing people's fear. Change is natural and good, but people's reaction to change is unpredictable and irrational. The result of learning how to manage change effectively is simple - the change is implemented.

Resistance and Fear of Change

Nothing is more unsettling to your people than change. Nothing has greater potential to cause failures, loss of production, or falling quality. Yet nothing is as important to the survival of your organization as change. History is full of examples of organizations that failed to change and that are now extinct. The secret to successfully managing change, from the perspective of the employees, is definition and understanding.

Resistance to change comes from a fear of the unknown or an expectation of loss. An individual's degree of resistance to change is determined by whether they perceive the change as good or bad, and how severe they expect the impact of the change to be on them. Their ultimate acceptance of the change is a function of how much resistance the person has and the quality of their coping skills and their support system.

As a leader, it is your job to address their resistance to help the individual reduce it to a minimal, manageable level. However, perception = reality, that is, the perception of an individual is their reality, which may be different to their peers, the manager, or others in the change process.

Change Equation

The following equation will assist in understanding what is required for change to occur and how managers and leaders can influence the change process:

$$D + F + I > CR$$

D = Dissatisfaction with the current state or process
F = Future appears better or more positive
I = Implement the change in small steps
CR = Change Resistance

A working example

A factory implements a change in production which will impact employees who currently are very happy with the way the product is produced. Management have decided on the change for speed of production which will in turn increase profitability.

For the factory management team they are **D**issatisfied with the current process, the **F**uture appears better because of higher production rates and increased profits. They have planned to **I**mplement the new process in what they consider to be in a non-invasive ways which will not decrease production, therefore these positive reasons tip the balance in favor of the change, therefore their **R**esistance to change becomes less and so change will occur without issue.

For employees, in the same factory example, their perception to the change may be different. They have little to no **D**issatisfaction to the current process. The employees on the production line have been working that way for many years and consider the process to be highly efficient already. When told of the change by the management team, the **F**uture looked uncertain, because with faster processing speed of product production, working hours may be reduced, causing insecurity in their jobs. When told of the change, the management team outlined a 30 day plan to **I**mplement the new process. Their head operator is on vacation during that time, resulting in a lack of training for that employee. When questioned about this, the management team brushed it aside, saying 'we'll deal with that person later', which caused others to become unsettled. These negative reasons caused the balance to be tipped where the negative reasons cause the Change Resistance to increase, therefore, change may occur, however resistance to it will be high.

Roles in Organizational Change

1 Change Sponsor - The person initiating a change

2 Change Agent - The person whose job it is to implement the change in your group

3 Change Target - The person who must add new skills or is asked to undergo change

RESPONSIBILITY FOR MANAGING CHANGE

The **employee does not have a responsibility to manage change** - the employee's responsibility is to continue to do their best in the face of change. This is different for every person and depends on a wide variety of factors (health, maturity, experience, personality, motivation etc).

Responsibility for managing change is with management and executives of the organization - they must manage the change in a way that employees can cope with it. The manager has a responsibility to facilitate and enable change, helping employees to understand the reasons for and objectives of the change. Increasingly the manager's role is to interpret and communicate, not to instruct and impose.

"Change must involve the people - change must not be imposed upon the people."

Complete Activity # 3
Managing Organizational Change - Case Study

ACTIVITY 3: MANAGING ORGANIZATIONAL CHANGE - CASE STUDY

The Catering Connection is a large manufacturer and distributor of catering supplies. Built on a family business and very conservative by nature, the company was purchased by an outside group, Catering Plus, when the founder decided to retire. Catering Plus immediately installed a new executive management team to develop a strategy for business growth and expansion.

Catering Plus saw an excellent opportunity to take advantage of The Catering Connection's basic product line by expanding into new markets and increasing the product offering. The production and operations procedures were immediately modified to accommodate product upgrades and the introduction of new and innovative products. New equipment was also enthusiastically purchased and installed to cope with the anticipated market demands.

In addition, new management introduced self-directed work teams into the manufacturing operations to facilitate greater employee participation and decision making in the production process. The restructure resulted in the redundancy of a number of production supervisors and the savings were reinvested in the upgrade of plant and equipment.

Unexpectedly, production declined.

In an attempt to resolve the problem, new management again reviewed production operations and implemented immediate changes to operating procedures and a rearrangement of manufacturing equipment.

Production continued to decline further.

ACTIVITY 3: CASE STUDY TASK

1. What potential employee issues did Catering Plus face in their purchase of The Catering Connection?

2. How well did Catering Plus handle the change process? Provide examples.

3. In your opinion, why did production decline?

4. What could Catering Plus have done differently to more effectively manage the implementation of change?

Now update your Learning Journal (page 77)

"

*"Ten years ago, Peter Senge introduced the
idea of the 'learning organization'.
Now he says that for big companies to change,
we need to stop thinking like mechanics and
to start acting like gardeners."*

ALAN M. WEBBER, LEARNING FOR A CHANGE

"

PLANNING CHANGE

PART 2

STRATEGIES FOR IMPLEMENTING CHANGE - THE 8 STEPS

Step 1 - Sound Preparation:

Clarify what the change is intended to achieve. Establish clear, measurable and realistic objectives and outcomes. Choose incremental over transformational change if time allows. Aim to introduce change fast enough to give a sense of progress, yet not exceeding people's ability to absorb and control it.

Step 2 - Create a Common Vision:

Help employees understand the need for change and provide a clear vision of what will be accomplished and how people will be affected.

Step 3 - Clear Communication:

Communicate the vision clearly, and often, to everyone. Establish processes to allow ongoing communication so that employees hear things through the official channels as opposed to the "grapevine".

Step 4 - Address Concerns and Enable Participation:

Develop processes to bring concerns out into the open and discuss them. Participation in the change process can help to develop ownership and commitment and improve its effectiveness - so build employee feedback into the change process. Where changes have negative consequences for individuals, provide support and assistance where possible.

Step 5 - Develop a Clear Action Plan:

Involve people in developing clear plans about who will do what, when and how in order to achieve the vision and make the change work.

Step 6 - Celebrate Progress:

Celebrate as stages are achieved to enable people to let go of the old and accept the new. Set short-term goals and provide a sense of achievement when they are reached. Aim to create a culture where change is about continuous learning and improvement and is viewed positively.

Step 7 - Create a Climate of Certainty :

Tell people what you do know, explain what will change and what will not. Establish processes to give individual and team feedback on how change is progressing, and how their efforts and support are helping. Do whatever you can to provide a sense of stability and routine.

Step 8 - Follow Up:

Monitor how the change is progressing and review the adequacy of risk controls. Establish what is working and what needs improving, and modify in the light of experience.

Complete Activity # 4
Strategies for Managing Change

ACTIVITY 4: STRATEGIES FOR MANAGING CHANGE

Match the following 8 Steps with the correct strategy for managing change and write in your own words a short summary (approximately 5-7 words) of each strategy.

STEP 1	Clear Communication	
STEP 2	Develop a Clear Action Plan	
STEP 3	Celebrate Progress	
STEP 4	Create a Common Vision	
STEP 5	Sound Preparation	
STEP 6	Create a Climate of Certainty	
STEP 7	Follow Up	
STEP 8	Address Concerns & Enable Participation	

Now update your Learning Journal (page 77)

STRATEGIC CHANGE IMPLEMENTATION WORKSHEET

Download this tool now. Starting on the next page, you have an opportunity to practice completing this tool for a real-life change management situation.

FREE DOWNLOAD

To download this tool go to
https://www.catherinemattiske.com/books
and follow the online instructions

 Download the **Strategic Change Implementation Worksheet** tool from
https://www.catherinemattiske.com/books

 **Tool Activity:**

- Working with a real life situation, complete this worksheet.
- Complete Steps 1, 2 & 3
  - Step 1 - Sound Preparation
  - Step 2 - Create a Common Vision
  - Step 3 - Clear Communication
- You will complete the rest of the tool later during this Learning Short-take®

PART 3
UNDERSTANDING YOUR EMPLOYEES

UNDERSTANDING YOUR EMPLOYEES

Change Perception

> **Definition:**
> Perception: A psychological process by which we make sense of what we are experiencing.

Perception: Whose idea was the change?

How hard is to adjust to change? Perhaps it depends on whether or not the change was your idea. When we decide to change, we usually jump in with both feet, excited about the possibilities that lie ahead. When change is forced upon us, we rebel. We look for every reason that the change imposed will not work.

What could happen if we learned to embrace change as a normal part of our lives and didn't fight with ourselves over it? It's our own perception of change that either holds us back or propels us forward?

Many of us have our own ideas on what is an acceptable change and what isn't. The truth is change happens to us everyday. People change everyday; they grow. Our circumstances change a little everyday as something new is thrown into the equation.

Yet, even though we intellectually know that change is constant, we fight to keep what is and what's familiar. If change brings us stress and discomfort, then there needs to be a change in how you respond to change. **Our response to change begins with our initial perception of the consequences of change.**

Perception Does Matter

If you move an employee's desk six inches, they may not notice or care. Yet if the reason you moved it those six inches was to fit in another worker in an adjacent desk, there may be high resistance to the change. It depends on whether the original employee feels the hiring of an additional employee is a threat to their job, or perceives the hiring as bringing in some needed assistance.

Looking beneath the surface

Your perception as a leader may not match that of the employee. The following table illustrates how leaders and employees perception can differ.

Perception Activity:

Do you see an old woman, a young woman, or can you see both?

On first glance...	Resistance...why? Perhaps one of these under the surface reasons...
A promotion is usually considered a good change.	An employee who doubts their ability to handle the new job may strongly resist the promotion. They will give you all kinds of reasons for not wanting the promotion, just not the real one.
You might expect a higher-level employee to be less concerned about being laid off, because they have savings and investments to support them during a job search.	The individual may feel they are over extended and that a job search will be long and complicated.
Your concern for a low-income employee being laid off.	The person might have stashed a nest egg in anticipation of the cut, or have a new job lined up.
Your best salesperson may balk at taking on new, high potential account.	This person may not want to take on the account, because they have an irrational feeling that they don't dress well enough, drive a good enough car, be confident to handle themselves at high level meetings etc.

CHANGE REACTION

Understanding The Change Matrix

The Change Matrix provides a valuable tool for identifying **where each of your employees are situated in the change process**, and for determining where you need to focus your energies to successfully managing change.

The Change Matrix identifies **four Stages of Change** that employees are likely to experience. However, it is important to recognise that employees will move through the stages at their own pace, according to their individual needs and perceptions. Your challenge as a leader is to support them through the change process, while at the same time meeting the needs of the organization for continued production and/or service.

The Change Matrix

	Passive in Change	Active in Change
Adopt new ways of doing things	**Observers**	**Enthusiasts**
Keep old ways of doing things	**Cynics**	**Blockers**

Stage 1 - Cynics: Passive in the Change Process/Retain old ways of doing things.

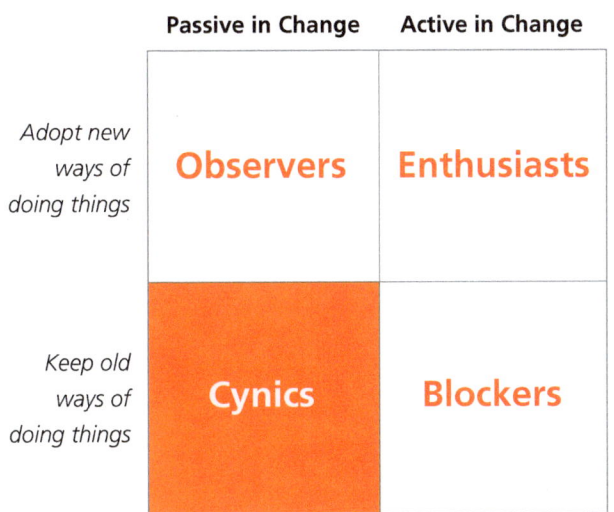

Cynics have a belief that nothing major is occurring in the organization. They either refuse to acknowledge major change or are seemingly unaware that things are or will be changing. It is important at this stage:

- To create an awareness of change for the individual.
- To ensure that the individual understands the need for change.
- Not to rush them through the process.

Stage 2 - Blockers: Active in the Change Process/Retain old ways of doing things.

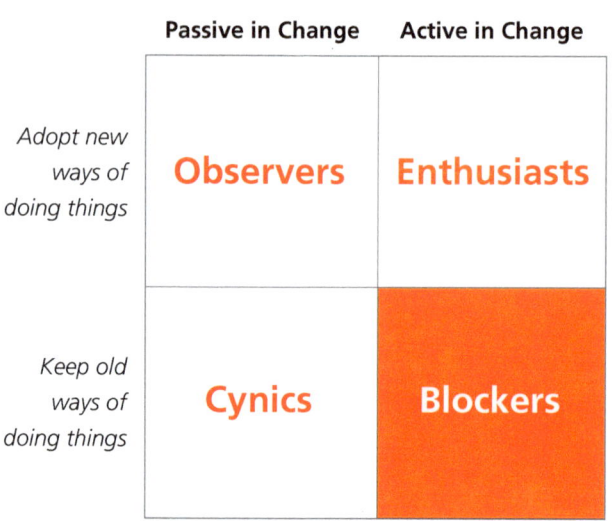

Blockers have a distinctly negative attitude towards change and will actively seek to oppose and sabotage change through work slowdowns, illness, irritability or sloppy performance. Generally their behavior is a result of fear of change. It is important at this stage:

- To acknowledge Blockers by affirming their right to resist. You don't have to agree, simply to acknowledge.
- To make it safe for Blockers to share their concerns.
- Listen carefully and ask clarifying questions to really understand their concerns.
- Explore whether issues raised are really a result of the change process or some other personal concern.
- Seek acceptance of the change process even if there is still unwillingness to agree with it.

Stage 3 - Observers: Passive in the Change Process/Will adopt new ways of doing things.

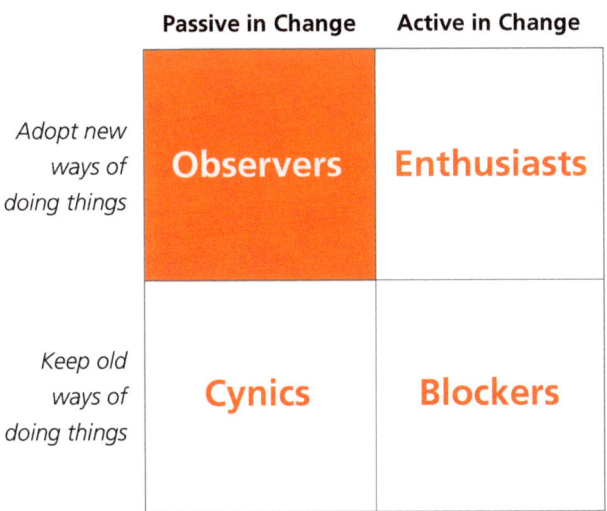

Observers begin to accept change and learn to develop methods to implement the change effectively for themselves and others. It is important at this stage to:

- Encourage creative thinking.
- Encourage Observers to set their own goals for success.
- Give Observers the opportunity to analyze the problem. Provide them with complete and accurate information.
- Encourage Observers to research, evaluate and make recommendations in relation to the change process.
- Reward Observers for their participation and assistance.

Stage 4 - Enthusiasts: Active in the Change Process/Adopt new ways of doing things.

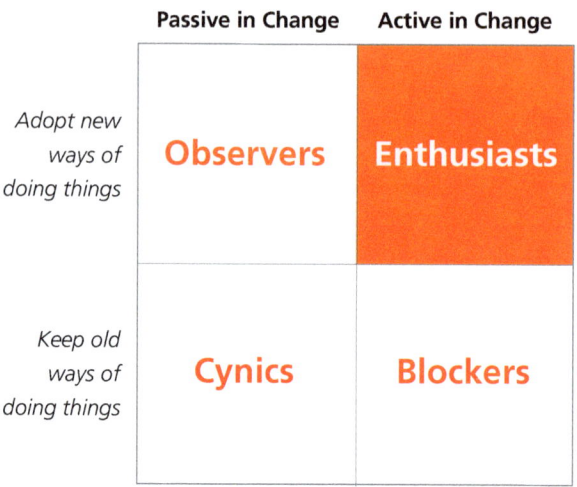

Enthusiasts are active participants in the change, make contributions and suggestions, initiate work on their own and come to see change for 'what it is'.

- Encourage Enthusiasts to become part of the change process.
- Assign them tasks and responsibilities within the new process.
- Allow them to coach and mentor other employees (with leadership guidance) who are still working through the change process.
- Provide opportunities for them to report on the success of early change strategies in meetings and other more open forums.

 **Complete Activity # 5a**
The Change Matrix - Assessing Employees

 **Complete Activity # 5b**
The Change Matrix - Plotting Employees

ACTIVITY 5A: THE CHANGE MATRIX - ASSESSING EMPLOYEES

Think of a real life situation. List your employees (or direct reports) names.
Using the grid below, identify whether they are Cynics, Blockers, Observers or Enthusiasts by placing a tick ✔ in the appropriate column.

Name	Cynics	Blockers	Observers	Enthusiasts

Now update your Learning Journal (page 77)

ACTIVITY 5B: THE CHANGE MATRIX - PLOTTING EMPLOYEES

Continue to work with the real life situation. Now plot employee names on the Change Matrix. Identify the quadrant in which the majority of your employees currently sit in the change process.

	Passive in Change	Active in Change
Adopt new ways of doing things	**Observers**	**Enthusiasts**
Keep old ways of doing things	**Cynics**	**Blockers**

Now update your Learning Journal (page 77)

SUCCESSFULLY IMPLEMENTING CHANGE

PART 4

THREE KEY CHANGE MANAGEMENT SKILLS

The following three skills, empathy, communication and participation are the foundation skills for managers and leaders when successfully implementing change.

Empathy

- To put yourself "in their shoes".
- What motivates them?
- What is happening to them personally?

Communication

- Create understanding about who, what, when and how things are occurring.
- Communicate the change by the best channel.
- Was your message clearly communicated.
- Right place, right time, in the right way.
- Did I receive effective feedback?
- What are my next steps.

Participation

Participate by:

- Appraise their own performance.
- Schedule their own time.
- Design improvements in the work flow.
- Assist in the decision making.
- Payoff is increased motivation and reduced negative behaviors such as slowdowns and failure to comply with standards.

Complete Activity # 6
Reflection Exercise

ACTIVITY 6: REFLECTION EXERCISE

Look at some ways you have previously managed change, complete the following reflection exercise. Recall an organizational change situation that you went through as an employee as opposed to a leader.

Briefly describe the change situation

_____
_____
_____
_____
_____

How was the change managed by the organization/your manager?

_____
_____
_____
_____
_____
_____

What did the organization/your manager do well in implementing the change?

_____
_____
_____
_____
_____
_____
_____

ACTIVITY 6: CONTINUED

What could the organization/your manager have done better in implementing the change?

_____
_____
_____
_____
_____

How did you feel as an employee in the change process?

_____
_____
_____
_____
_____

What was the outcome of the change process? Was it successful?

_____
_____
_____
_____
_____

What did this situation teach you about leadership in a change environment?

_____
_____
_____
_____
_____

Now update your Learning Journal (page 77)

CHANGE RESISTANCE

Dealing with Fear and Anger in the Change Process

Achieving successful organizational change entails thoughtful planning and sensitive implementation. Above all, it requires consultation with and involvement of the people affected by the change.

Those most impacted by change must agree with or at least understand the need for change, and have a chance to decide how the change will be managed. They must be involved in the planning and implementation of change. The organization cannot impose change - people and teams need to be empowered to find their own solutions and responses, with facilitation and support from managers, and tolerance and compassion from leaders and executives. Management and leadership style, and behavior is more important than clever process and policy.

Be mindful that the chief insecurity of most employees is change itself. Senior managers and directors responsible for managing organizational change do not, as a rule, fear change - they generally thrive on it. Remember that your people typically do not relish change, they may find it disturbing and threatening.

However, even where managers and leaders work actively to communicate and encourage employee participation and involvement in the change process, employees may still view any change with conflict, scepticism, negativity and disruption.

Employee anger and resistance to change can be triggered by many fears including:

- Redundancy
- Loss of Security
- Disorganization
- Loss of Status
- Ability to Cope
- Loss of Existing Relationships

In order to gain employee cooperation and allay fears you will need to:

- Highlight the way they will gain, benefit or avoid loss as a result of the change.
- Identify how the advantages of change will outweigh the disadvantages for each individual.
- Be prepared with suitable responses ready to address their concerns and uncertainties.
- Allow employee opportunities to share concerns, ask questions, and offer ideas and suggestions.
- Keep employees informed of what is happening.

Overcoming Resistance

Leaders can overcome the resistance by:

1. **Defining the change and**
2. **By getting mutual understanding.**

Don't try to rationalize things. It is not the best use of time wishing people were more predictable.

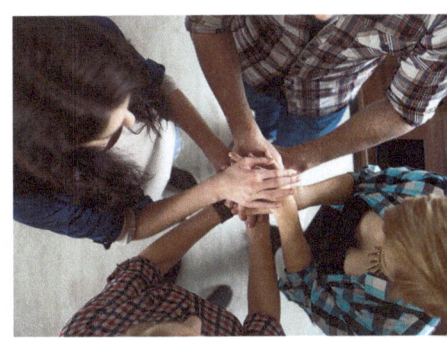

Instead, focus on opening and maintaining clear channels of communication with your employees so they understand what is coming and what it means to them. They will appreciate you for it and will be more productive both before and after the change.

1 - Overcoming Resistance through Change Definition

Leaders need to define the change for the employee in as much detail and as early as you can. Provide updates as things develop and become clearer.

In the case of the desk that has to be moved, tell the employee what's going on. "We need to bring in more workers. Our sales have increased by 40% and we can't meet that demand, even with lots of overtime. To make room for them, we'll have to rearrange things a little."

You could even ask the employees how they think the space should be rearranged. You don't have to accept their suggestions, but it's a start toward understanding.

Definition is a two-way street. In addition to defining the problem, you need to get the employees to define the reasons behind their resistance.

2 - Overcoming Resistance through Understanding

Understanding is also a two-way street. You want people to understand what is changing and why. Leaders focused on successfully implementing change also need to understand people's reluctance.

Effective leaders should help your people understand. They want to know what the change will be and when it will happen, but they also want to know why.

- Why is it happening now?
- Why can't things stay like they have always been?
- Why is it happening to me?

It is also important that they understand what is **not** changing. Not only does this give them one less thing to stress about, it also gives them an anchor, something to hold on to as they face the winds of uncertainty and change.

Effective leaders need to understand employee's specific fears.

- What are they concerned about?
- How strongly do they feel about it?
- Do they perceive it as a good or a bad thing?

 **Complete Activity # 7**
Preparing for Change Resistance

ACTIVITY 7: PREPARING FOR CHANGE RESISTANCE

List your employees (or direct reports) names. Using the grid below:
- Identify how they will gain, benefit or avoid loss as a result of the change that you need to implement.
- Identify the advantages versus the disadvantages of the change for each individual.
- Anticipate their concerns and prepare appropriate responses.

Name	How they will benefit as a result of the change	Advantages versus disadvantages of the changes	Anticipated Concerns

© 2022, TPC - The Performance Company Pty Limited. All rights reserved.

ACTIVITY 7: CONTINUED

Name	How they will benefit as a result of the change	Advantages versus disadvantages of the changes	Anticipated Concerns

Now update your Learning Journal (page 77)

WORKING WITH THE CHANGE MATRIX

PART 5

WORKING WITH THE CHANGE MATRIX

Applying Leadership Techniques

The aim for change leaders is to influence cynics, blockers and observers to become change enthusiasts. This section reviews each type of employee, and provides leadership techniques to encourage all employees to accept proposed change.

Organizational Cynicism - Background

In the organizational sciences, cynicism is typically viewed as an employee attitude that is detrimental to an organization.

Cynicism is generally believed to be a common employee characteristic. In a study by Kanter and Mirvis (1989) 43% of the American workforce were found to be cynical. Similarly, Reichers, Wanous, and Austin (1997) reported 48% of employees as being high in organizational cynicism. Therefore, the two studies, albeit eight years apart, delivered similar results.

One specific type of cynicism is organizational change cynicism (OCC). OCC is defined as "a complex attitude that includes behaviors resulting in increased beliefs of unfairness, feeling of distrust, and related actions against organizations".

"Employees who fail to see any improvement in their particular jobs from proposed changes direct their resentment toward the job itself by becoming dissatisfied and alienated."

ABRAHAM 2000

Change Matrix Model - Review

	Passive in Change	Active in Change
Adopt new ways of doing things	**Observers**	**Enthusiasts**
Keep old ways of doing things	**Cynics**	**Blockers**

Blockers & Cynics: Individual-Level Resistance

Using the Change Matrix, Blockers and Cynics display resistance to change. Blockers resist actively, while Cynics resist passively. Both Blockers and Cynics keep to their old way of doing things; therefore, they don't embrace the change. Individual-level resistance includes resistance to change due to uncertainty and insecurity, selective perception and retention, and habit.

"Blockers to change could be best overcome by getting those involved in the change to participate in its implementation."

LESTER COCK & JOHN FRENCH

Uncertainty and Insecurity

- Resistance due to uncertainty and insecurity occurs because employees **do not know what the outcome of the change will be.**

Selective Perception and Retention

- Resistance due to selective perception and retention occurs when **employees direct attention to how the change will affect their department, their function, or them personally.**

Habit

- Resistance due to habit occurs when employees are comfortable in their daily habits and **do not want to alter them due to change.**

Detecting Resistance

Cynics	**Blockers**

Keep old ways of doing things

Blockers and Cynics may have major issues surrounding loss of control, personal fears, loss of power or helplessness, loss, grief, risk, distrust, conflict, anger of a general emotional distrust of change.

There are three ways that employees may exhibit resistance to change:

1. Passive resistance,
2. Active resistance, and
3. Aggressive resistance.

Leaders may spot the symptoms of Blockers and Cynics, which may include:

- Reduced productivity
- Poor work quality
- Increased absenteeism
- Slowdowns or strikes
- Increased number of grievances
- Disengagement from manager and co-workers

Cynics

Passive Resistance

Passive resistance refers to negative feelings and opinions regarding the change. Signs of passive resistance may include agreeing verbally but not following through, feigning ignorance and withholding information.

Specific behaviors of Cynics may include the general symptoms (as above) plus:

- Can't find people when you want them
- Lack of contribution during meetings
- Not attending meetings
- Holding back information
- Delay or block messages or information
- Seem to block change while paying lip service to it

> *"Change has a bad reputation in our society. But it isn't all bad - not by any means. In fact, change is necessary in life - to keep us moving ... to keep us growing ... to keep us interested. Imagine life without change. It would be static ... boring ... dull."*
>
> DR. DENNIS O'GRADY

Blockers

Blockers may have major issues surrounding loss of control, loss of power or helplessness, loss, grief, risk, distrust, conflict and anger.

Active Resistance

Active resistance refers to actively opposing the change. Signs of active resistance may include strikes or increased absenteeism.

Aggressive Resistance

Aggressive resistance refers to behavior that actually blocks the change. Signs of aggressive resistance may include subversion or sabotage. Aggressive resistance is rare and can become dangerous. Therefore, aggressive resistance should never be allowed.

Specific behaviors of Blockers may include the general symptoms (as above) plus:

- Opposition to the project
- Argument and criticism in meetings
- Personal and emotional resistance
- Aggressive attitude
- Confrontation in discussions
- Unofficial opposition meetings
- Angry emails
- Threats of industrial action, and carrying out of those threats
- Conspiracies to stop change

Reducing Resistance to Change

Communication

Management must explain why the change is needed, identify the benefits of the change to individuals and departments, and be willing to answer all questions as they arise.

Topics regarding the change that must be covered are why, what, when, where, and how. Communication between management and employees can occur in the form of discussion groups, memos, formal reports, scheduled meetings, one-on-one meetings, etc.

Communication Verification = Understanding

The final step to education and communication is often overlooked. This step is verification of the message received. Employees should be asked to repeat the message they received, and management should compare the message received with the message management intended to send.

If there is a discrepancy between the message received and the message sent, then management should repeat the message until employees state a message received that matches the message sent. This step helps ensure understanding.

Education and communication is virtually useless without understanding.

7 ways to reduce resistance to change

You should anticipate resistance to change as the norm and not the exception. Your goal for change management is not to eliminate resistance, but rather to minimize the impact this resistance has on employees and the business.

The following ideas can help reduce resistance:

1. Involve interested parties in the planning of change by asking them for suggestions and incorporating their ideas.
2. Clearly define the need for the change by communicating the strategic decision personally and in written form.
3. Address the "people needs" of those involved. Disrupt only what needs to be changed. Help people retain friendships, comfortable settings and group norms wherever possible.
4. Design flexibility into change by phasing it in wherever possible. This will allow people to complete current efforts and assimilate new behaviors along the way. Allow employees to redefine their roles during the course of implementing change.
5. Be open and honest.
6. Focus continually on the positive aspects of the change. Be specific where you can.
7. Deliver training programs that develop basic skills as opposed to processes such as: conducting meetings, communication, teambuilding, self-esteem, and coaching.

TIPS & TRAPS OF MANAGING CHANGE

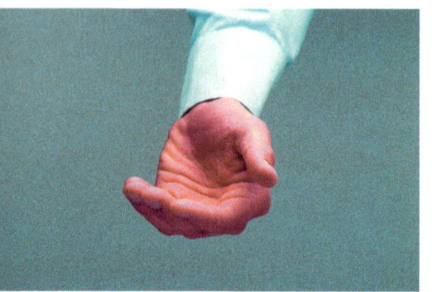

You can't draft people into change. They have to enroll.

Unless you are the CEO and in a position to compel people to perform, change is not a compulsory exercise.

In fact, even if you are the CEO, and theoretically in a position to compel people to perform, when it comes to change, you're liable to create your own worst nightmare: people quit, but stay; people say "yes," but do "no"; people go through the motions, but don't perform. (That's the Cynic described earlier in the Change Matrix.)

According to successful change agents, the key to making change happen is to create an environment where people gravitate in the direction you want them to go.

'Pull, don't push' allows employees to collaborate and making sure the company gets maximum benefit from their knowledge. Make people aware of best practices. They'll naturally use a better way if you make one available.

Remember dissatisfaction with the current process plus the future appears good plus implementation in small steps needs to be greater than the resistance to change (D+F+I >CR).

Focus on the 'business' part of 'business change'

The most important thing for change agents to remember is: it's just business. If you're going to get something done, you're going to discomfort people around you. You're going to interrupt routines, reveal problems and make more work on the way to making less work.

It's hardly surprising that the organization will push back. On the upside, occasionally it will be forgiving - if not cooperative - if you work like a professional. When it comes to change, sometimes it takes a leap of faith to get things going.

Change will no doubt create tension

Most managers are uncomfortable with what they don't know. Change leaders operate that way all the time. In a world that is changing with incredible speed, ambiguity is a constant. Ambiguity defines the work of the change agent: not a comfortable balance, but a dynamic tension between opposing forces. Change is all about taking people outside of their comfort zones. Change agents find themselves working simultaneously across the borders of conflicts - and almost always outside their own comfort zones.

Change agents have to be able to lead - and follow. They operate as insiders, working closely with teams - and also as outsiders, focused on making change happen. Change agents are simultaneously highly visible: willing to stand up in public to rally the troops, and genuinely invisible: turning the spotlight over to others when handing out credit is the best way to advance the cause. They need to be equally comfortable dealing with senior management and frontline workers - because a change agent needs the support of both groups. A change agent must always be in two places at once: where the organization is and where it's going.

You can't change the company without changing yourself.

In any change effort, the first person to change is you. It happens for two reasons.

First, once you begin to work as a change agent, you're automatically subject to a higher level of scrutiny and a tougher standard of judgment - from those both above and below you.

Second, to do the job means developing skills and techniques that immediately change how you work. Change and growth are linked.

It's true that many change efforts fail. And that most change agents feel squeezed, pushed, and pulled almost daily as they do their work of moving their team, their group, their company out of its comfort zone. And it's still the case that change agents who can master the skills make themselves the most valuable of all employees.

BUILDING AN ENTHUSIASTIC TEAM

Managing and Supporting Team Members

The goal of the Change Matrix is for the leader to influence Blockers, Cynics and Observers to become Enthusiasts in the proposed change. Unfortunately there is no 'magic wand' to create a team of Enthusiasts. However, using persuasion and influence aim to reduce resistance and reward those who are making the change.

	Passive in Change	Active in Change
Adopt new ways of doing things	**Observers**	**Enthusiasts**
Keep old ways of doing things	**Cynics**	**Blockers**

Responding to Observers

Passive in Change

Adopt new ways of doing things

Observers are making the change and adopting new ways of doing things. They are implementing the change, however they are passive. The aim of the leader is to influence the Observer to be more active in the change.

There may be a personal reason why Observers are making the change, yet are passive about it, including:

- Their personal and family situation (health, financial position, stability, mobility, relationships, etc.)
- Their professional career history and plans (successes, failures, promotions, aspirations, years left before retirement, 2nd career potential, etc.)
- The degree that this change will affect them personally (in some cases even large changes can have only a minimal impact on some employees)

Passive change by Observers does not mean that nothing is happening. It just means that adaptation is happening very slowly and with little or no influence from members of the organization. Things in the organization or the area in question just flow along like a lazy river with Observers in rafts with no paddles.

Ideas for Managing Observers

- **Discuss the change program.** Meet with the team member to discuss what happened during the learning program. Talk about what they have changed, and most importantly how the change links to their current role. Acknowledge completion of the change and reward their achievement appropriately.

- **Agree on goals.** If they have developed an Action Plan discuss the actions that they have listed. Ensure that the actions listed are relevant to their current role. If they have not developed an Action Plan, work side-by-side with them to create it. Working together on this will send a strong message of support to the Observer.

- **Monitor their progress** towards goal achievement. Ensure that barriers that may get in their way of achieving their learning goals are removed.

- **Stretch goals.** Where appropriate discuss ways of bringing the employee into the team. Perhaps partner them with a Blocker or a Cynic having them provide a buddy or coaching role. Alternatively, they could work on developing new work plans, procedures or policies by partnering with an Enthusiast. This form of co-operative learning may extend the Observer and may encourage their lower performing peers to increase their motivation for learning.

- **Discuss Support Mechanisms.** Talk about what support is in place for the employee and how they may access the support.

- **Review Progress and Provide Feedback.** Ensure that regular meetings are scheduled to check in on their progress. Continuously provide encouragement.

Responding to Blockers

Active in Change

Keep old ways of doing things

Blockers

Blockers can be disruptive, have irrational objections, however, at the very least they are active in the change, and generally the manager knows exactly who the Blockers are and what they think and feel. If opposition is openly stated and clearly visible, it is active resistance.

Ideas for Managing Blockers

Being able to interpret the behavior will assist leaders to choose the best response, which might include:

- In meetings, confront the issue and seek to alter their stance.
- In meetings, have a set time for negative (yet constructive) opinions and facts about the change.
  - Use de Bono's 6-Thinking Hats[1] to assist in the facilitation of this type of meeting, using the 'black hat' to bring out negativity in a constructive discussion.
- Use one-on-one meetings to find a compromise.
- Hold one-on-one meetings with key people who may be able to influence the Blocker.
- Set up small groups to tackle specific areas of concern.
- Listen sympathetically, then combine direct persuasion, subtle coaxing, and compromise (if possible) to bring them toward acceptance (not necessarily agreement) of the plan.

---

[1] Learning Short-take®: 'Creative Business Thinking' will assist you in learning more about de Bono's 6 Thinking Hats and other idea-generation and problem-solving techniques.

Responding to Cynics

Passive in Change

Keep old ways of doing things

Cynics

By contrast Cynics, keep to their old ways of doing things, but in 'public' (i.e. in front of the manager) are less likely to reveal that they are not implementing the change. During a change passive resistance can be just as effective as strident opposition. Successful change requires active collaboration.

Ideas for Managing Cynics

Being able to interpret the behavior will assist leaders to choose the best response, which might include:

- In meetings, investigate silence thoroughly.
- In meetings, have a set time for negative (yet constructive) opinions and facts about the change.
    - Use de Bono's 6-Thinking Hats to assist in the facilitation of this type of meeting, using the 'black hat' to bring out negativity in a constructive discussion.
- Have the cynic verbally agree and commit to the plan in front of others. (People are more likely to be consistent with their actions if they have voiced them to others).
- Seek verbalization of specific actions by each team member, including the cynic.
- Be straightforward when addressing concerns.
- Address specific fears about the future of individuals.
- Speak openly about what will change, and how that will affect people.
- Counteract negatively by being constantly upbeat and involving people in positive action.

Extending Enthusiasts

Active in Change

Adopt new ways of doing things | **Enthusiasts**

The Enthusiast already displays high levels of motivation towards the change and is actively implementing the change.

They have applied the change on the job and are comfortable in their ability to do it well. Enthusiasts may be coaching others in the team formally or informally. Due to their high level of motivation, they may explore more ideas about the change and implement their ideas autonomously.

The goal for Managers is to Extend Enthusiasts to achieve higher levels of performance.

Ideas for Managing Enthusiasts

- Reward Enthusiasts on their achievement. Rewards may be as simple as a private conversation or highlighting their uptake of new skills to the rest of the team in a team meeting, or a tangible reward, if appropriate.

- Agree on goals. Discuss their Action Plan. Ensure that each part of the change program has a relevant action item. Ensure that each action item links to their role and their current and future projects.

- Monitor their progress towards successful implementation of their Action Plan. Ensure that barriers that may get in their way of achieving their goals are removed.

- Stretch goals. Where appropriate discuss ways of stretching their Action Plan to further advancement. Perhaps partner them with a Blocker or a Cynic having them provide a buddy or coaching role. This form of co-operative teamwork may extend the Enthusiast and may also encourage their co-worker to increase their motivation for the change.

- Discuss Support Mechanisms. Talk about what support is in place for them and how they may access the support.

- Review Progress and Provide Feedback. Ensure that regular meetings are scheduled to check in on their progress. Continuously provide encouragement.

Complete Activity # 8
Managing The Change Matrix

ACTIVITY 8: MANAGING THE CHANGE MATRIX

1. Reflect on Activity 5b - The Change Matrix - Plotting Employees
2. Using the information in this section, brainstorm ideas for each employee to move them towards 'Enthusiast'. For those team members who are currently Enthusiasts, create strategies to extend their commitment and competence with the change.

Team Member Name	Current Change Matrix Plot (Enthusiast, Observer, Blocker, Cynic)	Ideas for areas of development

ACTIVITY 8: CONTINUED

Team Member Name	Current Change Matrix Plot (Enthusiast, Observer, Blocker, Cynic)	Ideas for areas of development

Now update your Learning Journal (page 77)

 Continue in your downloaded **Strategic Change Implementation Worksheet** tool from https://www.catherinemattiske.com/books

 **Tool Activity:**

- Working with a real life situation, continue and complete this worksheet.
- Complete the tool (Steps 4 - 8).
    - Step 4 - Address Concerns and Enable Participation
    - Step 5 - Develop a Clear Action
    - Step 6 - Celebrate Progress
    - Step 7 - Create a Climate of Certainty
    - Step 8 - Follow Up

A FINAL THOUGHT

PART 6

THE CROW AND THE PITCHER

Aesop (620-560 BC), known only for the genre of fables ascribed to him, was by tradition a slave who was a contemporary of Croesus and Peisistratus in the mid-sixth century BC in ancient Greece.

> A Crow, half-dead with thirst, came upon a Pitcher which had once been full of water; but when the Crow put its beak into the mouth of the Pitcher he found that only very little water was left in it, and that he could not reach far enough down to get at it.
>
> He tried, and he tried, but at last had to give up in despair.
>
> Then a thought came to him, and he took a pebble and dropped it into the Pitcher.
>
> Then he took another pebble and dropped it into the Pitcher. Then he took another pebble and dropped that into the Pitcher. Then he took another pebble and dropped that into the Pitcher. Then he took another pebble and dropped that into the Pitcher. Then he took another pebble and dropped that into the Pitcher.
>
> At last, at last, he saw the water mount up near him, and after casting in a few more pebbles he was able to quench his thirst and save his life.
>
> *The moral of this story is: Little by little does the trick.*

The Power of Change

Managing the challenge of change is a powerful responsibility. It is not easy and often it is expensive. However, failing to recognize the need to change and not working to build commitment to the change is far more costly. Making the investment of time, energy and money will benefit everyone: the employee, the management and the organization.

Advocates of change will enhance its implementation and installation. Employees with return your investment in them with increased productivity and personal growth.

Remember, you can effectively manage change. Moving forward while still preserving desirable aspects of the past is your challenge.

Section 2

LEARNING JOURNAL

The Learning Journal is used throughout the process to record your key learnings, hot tips and things to remember.

Update your Learning Journal at anytime. Ensure you complete your Learning Journal after you finish each activity. Then turn back to the Learning Short-take® to continue your learning.

LEARNING JOURNAL

As you work through this Learning Short-take®, make detailed notes on this page of the lessons you have learned and any useful skill areas. For each lesson or refresher point think about how you could further develop this skill. Your coach will want to discuss these with you in your Skill Development Action Planning meeting.

"…that is what learning is.
You suddenly understand something you've understood all your life, but in a new way."

DORIS LESSING

"Act as though it were impossible to fail."

WINSTON CHURCHILL

"The wise do at once what the fool does later."
BALTASAR GRACIAN (1601-58), SPANISH JESUIT PRIEST AND AUTHOR.

Learning or Idea	Action to be taken	Result Expected

Learning Journal - continued

Learning or Idea	Action to be taken	Result Expected

"Anyone who stops learning is old, whether at twenty or eighty."
HENRY FORD

Learning or Idea	Action to be taken	Result Expected

Learning Journal - continued

*"Everybody has accepted by now that change is unavoidable. But that still implies that change is like death and taxes -
it should be postponed as long as possible and no change would be vastly preferable. But in a period of upheaval, such as the one we are living in, change is the norm."*

PETER DRUCKER, MANAGEMENT CHALLENGES FOR THE 21ST CENTURY

Section 3

SKILL DEVELOPMENT ACTION PLAN

Your Skill Development Action Plan is the last Step in the process. After you have completed the Learning Short-take® and all Activities, update your Learning Journal, then complete this section.

SKILL DEVELOPMENT ACTION PLAN

This is the most important part of the program - your individual Skill Development Action Plan.

You need to complete this plan before meeting with your manager or prior to on-going coaching. You will discuss it in detail with your manager or coach as he or she will ensure that you have everything you need to complete the tasks and activities.

Once you have completed your **Skill Development Action Plan** schedule a meeting time with your manager or coach to review your plan. Take your Learning Short-take® and all other documentation received during the training course to this meeting.

Remember - you have committed to your **Skill Development Action Plan**, and need to make time to complete your tasks!

"The mind, once stretched by a new idea, never regains its original dimensions."

OLIVER WENDELL HOLMES

"Whatever you can do or dream you can - begin it. Boldness has genius, power and magic."

JOHANN WOLFGANG VON GOETHE

"Imagination is the eye of the soul."
JOSEPH JOUBERT (1754-1824)

Task or activity (Be specific)	Measure (this will help you to know you have achieved it)	Date (Be specific)
Reflect on your Learning Journal. Transfer action items that you can apply to your job. Ensure that you include some 'stretch goals' and also a blend of short, medium and long term goals.	Apart from you, who else is needed to assist you in achieving your goal.	Be specific. A general date such as 'Quarter 1', 'August', or 'by end of year' is vague and more likely to result in not achieving your target. Be specific – e.g. 22nd November.

IDEAS FOR DISCUSSION WITH MY MANAGER

Ideas

CONGRATULATIONS!

You've now completed this Learning Short-take®.

Meet with your Manager/Coach to discuss your
Skill Development Action Plan.

Suggested Reading

Leading Change. John P Kotter

The Heart of Change. John P Kotter, Dan Sa Cohen

Good to Great: Why some companies make the leap… and others don't. Jim Collins

Making Transitions: Make the Most of Change. William Bridges

> *"One key to successful leadership is continuous personal change. Personal change is a reflection of our inner growth and empowerment."*
>
> ROBERT E. QUINN

QUICK REFERENCE

This Quick Reference provides you with a summary of key concepts, models and reference material from Learning Short-takes®. We have also included some quotations to ponder.

Use this section as a quick reference to keep your learning active.

Quick Reference

> **The world doesn't fear a new idea. What it fears is a new experience.**
>
> DH Lawrence

Overview

Most often there is **strong resistance** to organizational change. People are inherently afraid of the unknown, are often **cynical about the application** of change, and may doubt that the change will accomplish the desired organizational outcomes. The best approach to address resistance is through **increased and sustained communication and education** throughout the change process. Employees need to be able to **trust** the organization.

Quick Reference

> **Change must involve the people - change must not be imposed upon the people.**

The Change Matrix

	Passive in Change	Active in Change
Adopt new ways of doing things	**Observers**	**Enthusiasts**
Keep old ways of doing things	**Cynics**	**Blockers**

Quick Reference

The Change Matrix

Stage 1 - Cynics: Passive in the Change Process. Retain old ways of doing things.

Stage 2 - Blockers: Active in the Change Process. Retain old ways of doing things.

Stage 3 - Observers: Passive in the Change Process. Will adopt new ways of doing things.

Stage 4 - Enthusiasts: Active in the Change Process. Adopt new ways of doing things.

Detecting Resistance - Cynics

- Can't find people when you want them
- Lack of contribution during meetings
- Not attending meetings
- Holding back information
- Delay or block messages or information
- Seem to block change while paying lip service to it

Quick Reference

Detecting Resistance - Blockers

- Opposition to the project
- Argument and criticism in meetings
- Personal and emotional resistance
- Aggressive attitude
- Confrontation in discussions
- Unofficial opposition meetings
- Angry emails
- Threats of industrial action, and carrying out of those threats
- Conspiracies to stop change

7 ways to reduce resistance to change

1. Ask team members for suggestions and incorporating their ideas.
2. Communicate the change personally and in written form.
3. Address the "people needs" of those involved.
4. Design flexibility into change by phasing it in wherever possible.
5. Be open and honest.
6. Focus continually on the positive aspects of the change.
7. Deliver training programs that develop basic skills.

Quick Reference

Responding to Observers

- Discuss the change program
- Agree on goals
- Monitor their progress towards goal achievement
- Stretch goals
- Discuss Support Mechanisms
- Review Progress and Provide Feedback

Responding to Blockers

Active in Change

| Keep old ways of doing things | **Blockers** |

- In meetings, confront the issue and seek to alter their stance
- In meetings, have a set time for negative (yet constructive) opinions and facts about the change.
- Use one-on-one meetings to find a compromise.
- Hold one-on-one meetings with key people who may be able to influence the Blocker.
- Set up small groups to tackle specific areas of concern
- Listen sympathetically, then combine direct persuasion, subtle coaxing, and compromise (if possible) to bring them toward acceptance (not necessarily agreement) of the plan.

Quick Reference

Responding to Cynics

Passive in Change

Keep old ways of doing things — **Cynics**

- In meetings, investigate silence thoroughly
- In meetings, have a set time for negative (yet constructive) opinions and facts about the change.
- Have the cynic verbally agree and commit to the plan in front of others. (People are more likely to be consistent with their actions if they have voiced them to others)
- Seek verbalization of specific actions by each team member, including the cynic
- Be straightforward when addressing concerns
- Address specific fears about the future of individuals
- Speak openly about what will change, and how that will affect people
- Counteract negatively by being constantly upbeat and involving people in positive action

Extending Enthusiasts

Active in Change

Adopt new ways of doing things | **Enthusiasts**

- Reward Enthusiasts on their achievement
- Agree on goals
- Monitor their progress towards successful implementation of their Action Plan
- Stretch goals. Where appropriate discuss ways of stretching their Action Plan to further advancement
- Discuss Support Mechanisms
- Review Progress and Provide Feedback

Quick Reference

Dealing with Fear & Anger

- Highlight the way employees will gain, benefit or avoid loss as a result of the change.
- Identify how the advantages of change will outweigh the disadvantages for each individual.
- Be prepared with suitable responses ready to address employee concerns and uncertainties.
- Allow employees an opportunity to share concerns, ask questions, and offer ideas and suggestions.
- Keep employees informed of what is happening.

Strategies for Managing Change - The 8 Steps

Step 1 - Sound Preparation

Step 2 - Create a Common Vision

Step 3 - Clear Communication

Step 4 - Address Concerns and Enable Participation

Step 5 - Develop a Clear Action Plan

Step 6 - Celebrate Progress

Step 7 - Create a Climate of Certainty

Step 8 - Follow Up

Quick Reference

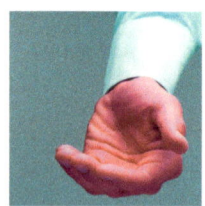

"You can't draft people into change. They have to enroll."

Change Agents

Change agents have to be able to lead and follow. They operate as insiders, working closely with teams, and also as outsiders, focused on making change happen. They are equally comfortable dealing with senior management and frontline workers because a they need the support of both groups.
A change agent must always be in two places at once: where the organization is and where it's going.

Quick Reference

"You can't change the company without changing yourself."

NEXT STEPS

Congratulations! You have now completed this Learning Short-take® title. In this section we have suggested Learning Short-take® titles for you that will build your learning.

You may view the entire list of these Learning Short-takes® at www.catherinemattiske.com/books. You can order them online here or from your bookstores.

The Effective Leader
Skills and Tools for Inspired Leadership

Learning Short-take® Outline

The Effective Leader will guide managers and leaders at all levels towards maximizing your effectiveness as a leader in the workplace. By demystifying the key concepts of communication, team building, leadership styles, individual and team motivation, performance, and interpersonal skills, you will be better equipped for success in your leadership role.

The Effective Leader includes covers both the essential theory and practical skills for successful leadership of teams. Through a series of self-assessment and action learning activities you will identify the differences between management and leadership, write a vision and mission statements, and identify your natural leadership style.
The Effective Leader will illustrate how to use additional leadership styles and how to plan and lead effective team meetings.

Increased leadership skills moves individuals and teams to increased resilience in the face of change, enhanced performance and greater success!

The Effective Leader includes the **Meeting Planner, Meeting Agenda, Core Essentials of Compelling Vision & Mission Statements Job Aid,** and the **Leadership Styles Summary,** provided as free downloadable tools.

Learning Objectives

- Define the relationship between leadership and management.
- Understand the meaning of vision, mission and values.
- Know the role of leader as coach.
- Apply the theory of the functional and situational approaches to leadership.
- Work on the personal qualities of leadership and display the will to lead.
- Have a high regard for communication in the leadership process and develop the ability to communicate.
- List ways to influence motivation for each member of your team.
- Create a Skill Development Action Plan

Course Content

- Part 1: The Effective Leader
- Part 2: Management vs Leadership
- Part 3: Leadership Vision & Mission
- Part 4: Leadership Styles
- Part 5: Understanding Behavior
- Part 6: Leadership & Roles
- Part 7: Leading a Team

Influencing for Opportunity
Identify and Maximize Ways to Influence

Learning Short-take® Outline

Influencing for Opportunity combines self-study with realistic workplace activities to provide you with the key skills and techniques to influence those around you. You will learn the theory of influence, influence principles and strategies, as well as how to plan and prepare for important opportunities to influence. As a result, you should achieve greater results in your organization, work more productively and effectively in a team environment, and develop stronger working relationships with co-workers, suppliers and customers.

The ability to influence others is critical in today's competitive business environment. Being highly skilled in influence enables you to build the relationships you need to get results inside or outside the organization. Employees and managers alike cannot assume they have power over others - they must earn it through influence. Being an influential person is a skill that can be learned and practiced. **Influencing for Opportunity** will help you succeed in the modern corporate environment by increasing your ability to influence others.

Influencing for Opportunity includes a **toolkit of job aids and learning support tools** provided to you as free downloads.

Course Content

- Part 1: Fundamentals of Influence
- Part 2: Influence: A Choice
- Part 3: Naturally Occurring Influence Patterns
- Part 4: Methods of Persuasion
- Part 5: The Challenges of Influence
- Part 6: Building a life of Influence

Learning Objectives

- Identify patterns of influence.
- Evaluate how you currently use influence behaviors and identify areas for development.
- Develop influence behaviors for greater personal and business success.
- Establish clear and powerful influence goals.
- Increase influence to overcome resistance.
- Describe how to ask for and receive support.
- Design an approach for formal and informal influence situations; apply the approach to a real-life situation.
- Create a Skill Development Action Plan.

Creative Business Thinking
Developing the Skills for Thinking Outside the Box

Learning Short-take® Outline

Creative Business Thinking includes a library of brilliant creativity tools, fun activities, and challenging business scenarios. These will help to stretch your thinking by deliberately challenging existing perspectives and considering alternative ways of working.

Creative Business Thinking is packed with techniques for creative thinking and fun 'mind quiz' activities. **Creative Business Thinking** constructively challenges the status quo to enable new ideas to surface and solve problems in ways that may not initially come to mind.

Within each of us there exists an infinite capacity for creating ideas and nurturing them through to innovation. **Creative Business Thinking** emphasizes pragmatic tools and techniques to successfully unlock creative potential.

Creative Business Thinking includes the job aid **15 Creativity Techniques for Problem Solving**, and the **Creative Business Thinking Techniques Wall Chart**, provided to you as free downloadable tools.

Learning Objectives

- Undertake a self assessment in creativity.
- List personal and organizational creative contributions.
- Choose personal creative techniques to be used in the workplace.
- Match group creativity techniques with case study applications.
- Use six thinking hats to solve a business challenge.
- Create a plan for an upcoming team meeting employing creative thinking techniques.

Course Content

- Part 1: Creativity and lateral thinking
- Part 2: Unleash those creative forces
- Part 3: Personal creative thinking techniques
- Part 4: Tools for Creative Business Thinking
  - 6 thinking hats
  - Brainstorming
  - Metaphors
  - Cause & effect (Fishbone Diagram)
  - Work breakdown structure
  - 5-Why's
  - Different point of view
  - Concept mapping / Mind mapping
- Part 5: Answers

www.catherinemattiske.com